QUESTIONS TO BRECHT

Thomas Strand

Library of Congress Cataloging in Publication Data

Strand, Thomas, 1944-
Questions to Brecht.

I. Title.
PS3569.T6912Q4 811'.5'4 75-19092
ISBN 0-914476-44-0

THORP SPRINGS PRESS 2311-C WOOLSEY STREET
BERKELEY, CALIFORNIA 94705

Table of Contents

VI, CHRISTMAS 1968

I wrote you
a poem once
because I thought
it was a debt
and I had always
wanted to write
you a poem
expressing things
that life could not.
I know now
that there can
never be a
debt between us.
We owe each other
more than words
and paper, more
than breath itself.
We owe each other
friendship to last
the Great Night
through.

moraira, spain, 1968

FORCED DEPARTURE

(for sheerie)

Seeing you
must have been like
the dazzlement of man on
earth's first summer.

And why is it, i wonder,
that when otherwise calm,
my hands tremble with you near?
It must be
that i love you.

Without each other
the world is a dark,
cold place and is nothing.

So say farewell gently,
softly, quickly,
i am fragile of heart
and my own tears
embarrass me.

How to pretend
that it doesn't really matter--

The very skies ache
with your going.

la grande, 1966

AN INTENDED LOVE POEM

autumn)

How shall i tell you,
my blue-eyed classic,
i am being another
and tired of this living?

I am to the dead skin pealing.
I am no longer of myself.

Sleep here, lady.
Next to me warm, sleep--
awake in the yellow cold,
beyond the embittered forest,
i shall find a way
at waking.

winter)

Deep in dark eyes,
in the rumpled bed
of the world--
it's quiet and lonely,
shadow and sorrow
and a choir of crickets
die where they sleep.

There are so many colors.
And so much murder
that it matters not
who's murdered
or who does the killing.

But there are so
many livings too
that one life
isn't enough
for one living.

spring)

Wherever i go
you surround me
no matter what corners
i glance from.

You like a vapor,
fragrance of incense,
smoke in water,
rising always rising,
the eternity of song.

You like the dance,
you as the dance,
unslippered, ivory ankled,
your nightgown tumbled
about your hips
in a sigh.

But why talk of love?
It is immeasurable.
Why talk of your hair
or thrust of leg
or rise of your breasts?
You are immeasurable yourself.

There is no end to you.
You are with me always
as my breath or my other self.
I cannot say i love you,
for what do i know of love?

I know the world
is softer with you.
With you i know
that i am God.

la grande, 1966/
portland, 1969

REUNION IN BERKELEY

These are for you.
I can only offer words.

You are one-third of my life at least.
You who have been gone these long weeks,
perhaps longer in the mind's eye,
but returning now in perpetual radiance.

You have brought me up.
For the weight of me,
endured the loss of queens.
For the child's ways of me,
suffered me to manhood.
You who bludgeoned, pleaded, prodded,
who brought me to myself,
who forgave me all my crimes,
who deserves nothing less
than a hearth
                    by the starry eye of God.

It is countless.
Journeys through portland, la grande,
san francisco--names of dreams,
exile to alabama, georgia, kentucky,
purge of fire in asia,
tacoma, depot street, exigence--
the fragrance of you
still on my towel.

And when asked by my unborn daughter
if we grow still
from seperation, from loss,
i shall tell her no.
There is no end to the trespasses of the heart.
It contains undrempt, nameless things.
It grows large
with each day, and each new love,
with each stranger's face,
with each crack in the wall.

It must be so

It must be so

berkeley, 1967

"RIVER OF BLOOD"

When are you bastards
going to realize that a man
grows old and dies just the same?

Perhaps rivers of blood
is what it takes to waken the white community.
I once knew a poet,
black as obsidian,
and with him walked the streets of Nashville
until we nearly dropped
to find a place where we could talk
of poetry and love.

Nothing
is black or white
but golden!

berkeley, 1967

from the book Rivers of Blood, Years of Darkness by Robert Conot.

REFLECTIONS OF A WOUNDED CORPORAL

Across the green rice fields
filled with human dung
the young Vietnamese sniper
glared at me.

He was about to impress me
on the merit of communism.
I was there to learn the dirtysonofabitch
about the right of democracy.

So when he shot me;
not once, not twice, nor thrice
but four
          (he wasn't easily satisfied)

I wonder what was in his mind
when he saw me flounder like a stricken whale
a broken dog.

berkeley, 1967

PATTERNS

when he was still a child
his father beat the mother to a pulp
and raged into the dark
to be knifed down by a beer truck.

he was subsequently raised
by his brokennosed mother who
had baseball knuckles from laundry detergents.

at 15 he was seduced by
a neighbor who had come
over to borrow five dollars.

at 18 underwent
a horrible ordeal of
self-examination and decided
to study law at all costs
though it cost his mother
and a strawberry girl who loved him.

at 37 he was solvent.
at 38 a married man
(happily)
and a spankin' new daddy.

he raised his son to play football
and shoved him into west point
and had sent 97,486 hard-core criminals to prison
(mostly for life).

at 63 his wife slashed her wrists.
at 71 he took four strokes
in half as many days
(bravely)
which left him paralyzed from the eyes down.
he was stunned but not out.

at 77 he drowned
when his wheelchair got away
and sped like lightning
down a hill to san francisco bay.

after the funeral
his son, the lieutenant-colonel,
was never heard from
(again)
.

berkeley, 1967

SUNDAY MORNING

I set right to work.
Put the bottle on the stove.
Whipped off the soggy diaper,
a drop of oil and pinned on the new.
Shoved the bottle into his fat mug,
kept him awake until he finished every drop.
Burped his little tummy--
which put him to sleep.
Changed his untimely pants again--
which woke him up.
Then began the slow process of sleep,
patting his rump in a rocking chair
that creaked like an old ship.
He won't remember my inflated head,
my jangled hands,
the two burnt-out suns behind my eyelids.
Ah, no, me bucko--lie quiet.
This is a fragment that
even you don't own.

berkeley, 1967

DOWN AND UP THE WEST COAST

(for kell & betsy robertson)

I.

It was the final act of bitterness
toward the town of my youth
when we fled in the dread of winter,
hangover quick, to San Francisco.
The car sagged like a broken horse,
my books piled atop, Kell's guitar
beneath the beer, Betsy's junk stacked
to the windows, the back seat where
their child of three months
rode dry-eyed, unwhimpering.
We sped at thirty miles an hour
down the highway, a road
so long traveled that I knew each bend,
so long traveled with my thumb out.
The lonesome old friend of a road,
speeding and drinking all the way--
they afraid as I was
that I'd lose my guts
and sentence us all to worn-out Portland.

The night there in
a slumber of beer and wine.
Three adults in the front, cramped and fogged.
The child hardly noticed in back.
Rain a fifth passenger.
Portland was a guillotine to me,
a roadblock of skeletons.

But once we got by--
a straight shot south on Highway 5,
down past Albany where
the police stopped us
and kept stopping us
because we looked like migrant labor
and theives and dope addicts, God knows what.
Because the tail light was out,
because the old Chevrolet looked stolen
or forged from a graveyard.

For the first time we planned--
not to chance Grant's Pass road
frozen stiff and deadly
but flow west to the Pacific
to the unlikely town of Drain
where we talked of dwarves and gnomes.
To Reedsport, south, down the map
falling like a waterbead.

Left Brookings to Humbug Mountain,
rain shrouding us, a vice of fog,
the right side disappearing into
a bleakness we knew as the sea.
Outside the door, a drop
swift to the rocks and tide.

Pavement narrowing to a needlepoint.
Struggling at five miles an hour
on a grade where a goat would shy.
Cars crowding us over, honking us on.
Eager to sign papers, they passed
us with a black curse,
drenched us in spray from tail pipes.
Then down Humbug Mountain
sliding over a bridge where
golden bears welcomed us
to the rich mud of California.

The last leg in San Rafeal,
a barkeep wished us warm and safe.
And rain, rain enough to drive us mad.
Rain enough that I didn't notice
when we were on the Golden Gate
crossing to the city of dreams.

II.

A whirlwind trip to Tacoma,
taken in one breath,
back to my bride, my wife,
blood of my poems.
Miles closer and miles white
falling away like ashes
from a dead man's thumb.
The car crumbling to tatters beneath me.
But it was all right.
Even her family was all right.
Even I not knowing how to act
around a family. Even the ritual.
Even the last consummation of our love.

III.

We met you then in the city
where you had found us a roof.
A home we had to fashion for ourselves.
Love in me so long unborn,
forgotten, a hard thing to free.
I noticed that I didn't talk much,
agreed with most everything.
That I looked sad most of the time
was not so. Believe me.
It was a fear of life, of myself.
My confusion with anything so human,
so warm.

Warm as roots
fresh dug
of the earth.

berkeley, 1968

SHADE AND SORROW

There you sit.
And though it doesn't stop with you,
you are the beginning
of all my trials and pain.

You are judgement, a circular court,
the gallows, the knife
falling from an immeasurable height.
You are lawmaker, dust of fate

in the dark wind of nations.
You are Avarice, you are Pride.
You have brought civilization
all this way from the Dark Ages.

The punishment is more humane,
less likely to turn the stomach
or the unwary head toward
your soul in shadow.

I have learned long ago
to hold my tongue.
But I am not dead yet.
Still, I do not condemn you.

I do not pity you.
You leave me cold as a corpse.

berkeley, 1967

GENESIS

I am sitting on a vacant star
watching God put the world together.

His long arm reaches out over everything
to grab an asteroid here, a bit of eternity.

He rolls His big flat hands
as a child with a snowball.

He breathes air into frail clay figures
that could better be used

as targets in a shooting gallery,
exchanged for stuffed lions.

Somewhere He crosses the wires
and fills space with a frenzy of sparks.

From my cosmic height
my legs dangle on a keen star-edge

deep into a far nothingness
and watch the spectacle begin.

berkeley, 1968

WE GO QUICK

We go quick
out of the shouting rain
that gashes the guts out of dublin.
We sit counting our coppers,
enough for tea at least,
so they won't toss us out
onto the damp cobblestones.
I sit wondering:

when will she
start bleeding again
or perhaps she will
be perpetually pregnant

perpetually running the cycle
around st. steven's green
along with horse drawn carts,
the vanished statue of archibald william
and the stench under o'connell bridge.

Remember now:
go quick!

dublin, 1968

ONCE MARCO POLO

Once marco polo
   went so far
      east
that he was damn near
   west.

Then it got
   to be my turn,
      and i drifted around
here and there
   trusting (mostly)
      to God.

It was as if
   the entire universe
      was in flux
with demented
   wings.

Everyone in transit.
   Jetsam everywhere.
      And i awoke in amsterdam
not really remembering
   how i managed
      it.

oxford, 1969

JEREZ

In a prayer of night
our bodies whispered together.
And as my hand smoothed
a circle of her warmth, she said--
a woman is composed of curves.
A man is of lines.
Lines that spirit the seed
into woman's soft glove of flesh.
Lying thus, in a brace of stars,
my pulse is barely moving.
Roads and deserts are delusion.
There are only meadows:
let us go and lie in them.

moraira, spain, 1969

"RAGING IN THE DARK"

--W. B. Yeats--

I own nothing.
   Not what i buy
or the money i use.
   Not the air i breathe
or the land i walk
   nor the body i stand up in.
I do not own my life.
   I do not own my soul.

I have swallowed
   deep the hook.
Thrash on the line.
   Go and thrash on the line.

I shuttle through the world
   in a chain gang.
I exist fast in fetters,
   the links rattling loose
in my head. I may move,
   but from one bondage
to another--jellyfish
   nailed to a plank.

Thoughts are not mine.
   Neither my blindness.
Nothing is mine. Not
   even the final ashes.

The noose is always.
   I slip it about the throat
with my deft left hand.
   The hand i do not own.

These burning words should burn.
   The sperm should dry and choke.
The spaces in my mind
   needs rockets for travel.

I should not talk
  or write. I should
be nothing. It has
   its own reward.

I rage to an empty sky.
   I cry to deafness.
Only pain kills the pain
   and i am beyond despair.

Impotence is my anger!
   I am calmer now.
Terror remains.

moraira, spain, 1969

TRAIN OUT OF OXFORD

She sits ignoring me.
A Woman's Magazine is plained out before her.
Her fingers sparkle with gold rings
as she turns the pages.
Her blond hair fluffs about her angel's face.
England files by beyond her, out the window.
Her polished legs cross and recross,
the smoothness rubbing against
my soiled jeans.
I think how nice it would be to nail her.
She has such perfect teeth.
Her skin is scented and scrubbed.
I'd take her like an animal.
Mount her like bull in field.

But it isn't worth it.
It's just the pervert in me urged
to the surface by such a sight.
She glances at me. My eye catches hers.
She quickly returns to her True Love story

She's young. She's pure.
She's scented and scrubbed.
She's beautiful and lean
and us together for a moment
would be fine.

The poet would say:
"Her brains are in her tits!"
But better that
than no brains
and no tits either.

oxford, 1969

EUSTON STATION

Euston   Euston
sound of a locomotive
in a spasm of time.

I come up to you,
a bit of rubbage
spat from your bowels.

Euston   Euston
eight days i have slept hard
on your scoured face.

Even here the black man
gets the shit end of it
or maybe especially here.

Euston   Euston
i'm down on haymarket
with all this cunt and money

walking around me.
A lot of blood's
gone under the bridge.

Euston   Euston
i dodge your blue police
and harvest butts from the floor.

The irish boys fart to each other,
your ashen gangsters are on to me--
the tramp in the rain.

Euston   Euston
a million muddied feet
pass me up

and when i leave--
england will flicker by
like an old dirty film.

london, 1969

SOMETIMES FRIENDSHIP

I once stayed
in a men's hotel
where a young, twisted
spastic had residency.

He would waylay me
at six in the evening
to jaw about laser beams,
the art of the bullwhip,
all the girls he had loved
in his mind--any damn thing.

It would be three
or four in the morning
before i could escape.

He used to trap me
into reading to him,
armed with an invalid's cunning
that it's impossible
to refuse men in wheelchairs.

He would roll his busted
gnarled body down the hall
to knock timidly at my door.
I'd read him Superman comics
until i passed out with sleep.

Sometimes he'd convince me
that i would be christian
if i'd push him down
to the street.

On sixth avenue
he'd sit to watch the world--
to love all the girls
of his mind.

I am cautious now,
whenever i leave my room to shave.
And after six in the evening--
i don't answer the door.

portland, 1970

THIS MOST PERFECT OF NIGHTS

who can think of death and madness
on this most green of nights

who can defile this grace
who has the voice to betray

the earth is the heart of God
and it lies wounded, wounded

on this most gentle of nights
life has no time for death

portland, 1970

ASTRONAUTS GET LOST ON EARTH

"Well, by God," he said.
"Somebody finally showed us
where we are!"

The old tramp and I
were standing by the corner
drugstore where they displayed
an exclusive photograph
of the world taken from
the surface of the moon.

Labels were stuck here & there
on its proud, glossy face.
One arrow pointed out
the North American Continent.

The tramp (his fly unzipped
& stinking of puke & wine,
age breathing from behind
his stubble of broken memories)
stood with me for a moment.

"Hell," he said.
"It don't look
like much to me."

portland, 1970

THE OLD MAN

The old man
with secrets in his hands
refuses to tell.

He sits into long afternoons
never stirring, never betraying himself,
never revealing the morning
that passed through him.

The people say he's harmless,
that his children
never wanted him,
and that his wife was in fear
for his soul.

And the old man
with secrets in his hands
refuses to tell.

ashland, 1970

TRYST

Her father got off
work at midnight,
so they had to hurry.

His hand trembled,
clumsy with sweat,
and was the shy one
when both of them
were finally bare
standing before themselves.

He, the quickening seducer;
she, the silent receptacle,
guiding him between
her pale thighs.

But he was urgent,
hurting her,
rising too fast for her,
and there was much blood
which they hadn't expected.
And they felt somehow cheated.

It wasn't anything
like they had supposed.

She put clean sheets
on the bed and fixed
her father a light meal.

And when the old man came in,
choked with factory grease,
he fell across a dream
of his year dead wife

on the bed where
everything had begun
to change.

ashland, 1970

HURRAH FOR THE HUMAN SPIRIT!

Hurrah for the human spirit!

The march of it begins nowhere
and ends everywhere.
We cannot stop it.

To try would be more difficult than hope,
more difficult than infinity,
as difficult as finding
someone to love.

Hurrah for the human spirit!

Though we try to gun it down
and club it back,
we can do nothing.

It's a bigger job than happiness,
bigger than reason,
a bigger job than making sense
out of the world.

Hurrah for the human spirit!

ashland,1970

SANDERSON CREEK INCIDENT

Life was a pretty thing
before we got hold of her.

although she lay at the bottom
of sanderson creek road,
her dress thrown over her head,
dripping blood to the ankles,
three bullet holes in her face,
and the back of her head
making a fine looking stew--

Life was a pretty thing
before we got hold of her.

although what was left of her
was discovered by two small boys
who suddenly lost their wonder,
although, since that day,
the people of sanderson creek
never again wept,
and no one ever died,
or ever again thought of each other--

Life was a pretty thing
before we got hold of her.

ashland, 1971

AMNESTY

(for jeanna)

This is a day like all days
except we do not hate.
The cosmic alarm has failed.
A counsel of stars has seen fit
to grant a day of grace.

Everything is shelved
including Christmas and poetry.
Nothing proceeds or exists
but a vast pause and look.
This is a day when
the world is forgiven.

Living creatures proclaim
a truce from the hunt,
the phallic expression of land
enters the folds of the sea

and the soft burning of the moon
guarantees my life.

ashland, 1971

THE CONCENTRATED MOMENT

Oh, the gods and stars do envy us
   and all the devils too.

The concentrated moment.
Your beauty more lasting
   than the moment.
Everything of you more lasting
   than time or trouble.

Your body
   a thousand times your body,
   your body flowing, moaning,
   your body with me, beneath me moving.
Your hair falling
   in a flash of dark.
Your eyes shinning, sighing,
   rising to mine.
Your eyes in fathoms of green.
My hand churning you.

My mouth on your legs.
Your parted smooth legs bending,
   pumping, folding rightly.
My face in your rise of fur.
My hands traveling your belly,
   tongue circleing in you,
   teeth pulling at your tips.

Your breasts given me.
The orbital womanness.
You holding them to me,
   tracing their outline,
   nipples jutting hard as I.
If only they were fed with milk,
   running over us now
   in a kind of benediction.

Your hands strong on me.
Your breath quick in my ear.
My hands curved beneath
   your curve.
Your hand cupping me,
   legs urgent on me.
My breath turning liquid
   in your hair.

We are hard upon each other.
Saturated with our own tremors,
   there is no altruism
   among lovers.
A sudden spasm and lunge
   into a protracted shuddering
   and then at rest.

We lie back stunned with effort.
We look beyond ourselves,
   into each other.
Our bodies cool like the night.
We embrace, entwine,
   loving past the moment.

I brush the net of hair
   from your face
   and seek to hold you,
   enfold you.

Oh, all the stars and gods do envy us
   and devils too.

ashland, 1972

THE HOUSE THAT WE BUILT

Because i live in a house

Because i live in a house
filled with a beautiful woman

Because i live in a house
filled with a beautiful woman
and everything around me mine

Because i live in a house
filled with a beautiful woman
and everything around me mine
and have no problems but those we create

Because i live in a house
filled with a beautiful woman
and everything around me mine
and have no problems but those we create
the created misunderstandings of tomorrow

Because i live in a house
filled with a beautiful woman
and everything around me mine
and have no problems but those we create
the created misunderstandings of tomorrow
and the insanity we use to live

Because i live in a house

Because i live in a house
filled with a beautiful woman

Because i live in a house
filled with a beautiful woman
and i lie abed amorning dreaming

Because i live in a house
filled with a beautiful woman
and i lie abed amorning dreaming
her breathing traveling through my brain

Because i live in a house
filled with a beautiful woman
and i lie abed amorning dreaming
her breathing traveling through my brain
her body tuned to a fine song

Because i live in a house
filled with a beautiful woman
and i lie abed amorning dreaming
her breathing traveling through my brain
her body tuned to a fine song
i lean to touch her stillness

Because i live in a beautiful house
filled with woman

ashland, 1971

THE WOMAN BESIDE ME

The smooth red headlines of the sun
   hang in the delicate air.
She sleeps in the antique light,
   hair falling darkly down,
   the sweat of her legs against me.
Awake & turning to her:

She is made of what
   i am made of.
Her flesh is as fragile
   as my own.
Her bones can be as easily
   broken.
Her blood courses as
   my blood courses.
She can be as foolish as i,
   as selfish as i,
   and as cruel, as lost.
Her wounds are as apparent
   as mine, wounding each other.
She is composed of the same circuits,
   energy, infrastructure.
What, then, explains this question?
She stretches before me,
   an extension of infinity.

I rest near her now.
Inside, the darkness of the night
   is intricate.
Outside, the sun slips down
   beyond the circumference of God.

ashland, 1972

DEPARTURE AND ARRIVAL: THE INTERIM

You have been gone eight days.
You will be gone fifteen.
Ages.
I think of the things not said,
of things I did not make firm,
things I should have repeated
again and again, over and over
like an anaphora
until you were sick of hearing them,
until they fused themselves
in your brain like another synapse.
This gnawing: that you could have gone
without knowing that I love you.
If I could have burned it into your flesh,
I would have.
If I could have conditioned you
to remember it every third breath
like one of Pavlov's dogs,
I would have.
If I could have reached you by telepathy
and began again the telling,
I would have.
I can only wait on your return
so I can begin again the litany.
Now I am cut off, in a vacuum.
No letters, no telephone.
I can only shout into the muted night:
Remember, damn you! Remember.

ashland, 1972

JOURNEY WITHOUT DESTINATION

My love went riding,
green and wintry,
out of grace,
out of her station,
out of the boundries
that bound her.

Into that sullen unknown
went she riding,
into the error of tomorrow,
the brooding weather of mind,
into the sharp, descending
corners of her heart.

She left behind
those who thought they knew her,
locked in their own grimaces,
those rejected flagmen
not earning their wages,
those who could not also descend.

It's a journey without destination,
one with a mean bastard down there.
But she won't run his errands
and she won't kiss his ass
or wait for him to decide
when he's going to strike.

There's a thought down there
that she's not seen
and a woman she doesn't know.
Into the light and terror
my love went riding,
green and wintry.

ashland, 1972

END OF THE ENDING

The sallow fringe of sky
struggles through the panicked snow.
I sit with a coffee cup,
the clatter of cafe,
voices tumbling about me.

"It doesn't make any sense sometimes.
Not the act, but the saying of it,"
you said.

What is this thing,
this love that makes
a man act hateful?
You are my axis.
I revolve about you.
All I want (and all you want)
is a look, a touch, an appreciation,
to make sure that I am still alive,
to be sure that I am not
just a dungcake to be plowed
into the rich soil of your past.

"It doesn't make any sense sometimes.
Not the act, but the saying of it,"
you said.

I struggle through the geometric town,
the tangled snow, the vague night
where there are no answers,
where you are in every shadow.
Great God! How much
do I cost myself?

ashland, 1973

THE PAST IS NEVER AS DEAD AS YOU KILLED IT

All the women of the world
are of scant match for you.
Yet I must be content with them.
I love them, love all of them,
love their moves and graces
but carry your history
always in my eyes.

Love is not nearly dream.

That last time my voice
was an execution,
my footsteps a closing door,
and I panicked into the dim morning.

Now a death could be on hand
for both of us,
some unknown stranger
waiting to lead us
away from ourselves.

When we at last be what we are,
I want to come near you
and begin belief again.

ashland, 1973

TO HER: IN PARTING

How far we have come,
now that the rain-streaked leaves
hover about the faded landscape
that looks like a fresh-dipped watercolor.

There is no anger here, not even bitterness.
Though much has been failure, much treasonous,
the world still pounds out its coinage
as someone, somewhere finds himself again.

Tomorrow grows fat in the sky
and Fate has no duty here anymore.
Solution lies with God no longer
but with us.

REFLECTIONS ON READING HOMER

The trouble with civilization,
among other things,
is that there's just too goddamn
much being written.
Everybody I know is a writer.
Or opinionated enough to be one.
There's millions of them around
like little ants.
You can't say "nymph" or "sprite" or "gay"
or anything like that anymore.
Think what a problem Nietzsche would
have today with a title like *Ecce Homo*!

It's a very limiting thing.
A fellow could go nuts trying
to think of something to say that
the newspapers haven't already ravaged.
I can't imagine anybody getting
excited about sex anymore.
Alienation is passe.
Everybody knows that the government
is a bunch of graverobbing shits.

That old fart Homer had it made.
There weren't many people
around then that could read,
never mind write.
His position was assurred.
It didn't matter if what
he wrote was so much slop.
That it existed was enough.
A matter of historiography.
I doubt if he worried much
about his critics
or of finding a publisher.
Besides, war novels were new then.
In fact, war itself was new.
Comparatively.
Think of the gallons of blood
that have been spread around since then!
War's a ho-hum business these days.

At the present rate of exchange,
I doubt if even going blind
would help a hell-of-a-lot.
To write a book, Trumbo had to lose
his eyes and ears and arms and legs
and tongue and cheek and . . .well,
as much as possible and still be alive.
Even at that, the book
was ignored for fourty years.
Frankly, if you have to go through
all that to write a book . . .
it just isn't worth it.

One of these days, I'll pass on.
Maybe end up in Limbo where Dante
says all the literati go, a place
not unlike the elephant's graveyard.
Maybe I'll meet up
with that lucky bastard Homer.
Buy him a beer.
See what he has to say.

Until then, I just park myself
on a little knoll somewhere
dreaming up at a star
the astronomers haven't discovered yet,
and find my own winter and spring.

ashland, 1970

END BRAIN

in the last effort of sky
   the rain comes down like memories

the night blooms before me
   a black rose of night

i stand in the little dark
   that patiently fills
the edges of the earth
   the little dark
that stands in my brain

i move among these padlocked houses
   with wars separating them

somewhere a dog barks
   as if he sensed eternity

someone on the next street
   stirs in shadow
threatened by himself

beyond these walls that men
   have killed for
people twist in their dreams

i feel the beating rise
   out of my own
padlocked heart

and even the fear
   is beautiful

ashland, 1971

ONLY BE WOMAN WITH ME

only be woman with me

without your gentle beauty
there could be no poetry
without your hair gratefully falling
there would be no art

you fill that which is nothing
as life augments life
as the artist does not exist
without the agony of love

culture is there in the womb
and i am here but in imitation
come near me now
write me something with your difference

be only woman with me
add earth to bone
and flesh to soul

ashland, 1971

WASTE IS THE WORST OF THE NATURAL ELEMENTS

". . .I conclude now I have no
inner resources, because I am heavy bored."

--John Berryman--

I have totally wasted the day.
I can't undo what I've just undone.
It's gone; pissed away; rotted away.
It's killed; buried; a tombstone's on it.

It is 3 AM and a freight train passes the house.
Its travel is loud and distanced.
The windows rattle; it threatens entry.

The wind outside harks back to nothing.
I am alone with the little of my life.
I sit and stare into my own depression.
My hands are idle; hating each other.

I cannot work; I cannot think.
I cannot love, I've tried.
I've tried but cannot scarcely live.

I conclude then that I am a modern
American, beset with modern ills.
I suffer from an evil in the bloodstream,
a hunger in the brain.

I realize that this is but a momentary thing;
yet I cannot rid the thought
that death is a good idea.

ashland, 1972

CONVERSATIONS YOUNG AND OLD: A PLAY

Look, I can understand how you feel.
Nobody likes to do these things, after all.
It's not as if I liked World War II any better.
You just don't understand the issues.

(But Father, they're killing children).

Hey, listen. Take it from me. Trust me.
I've lived a lot longer than you have.
I've had more expierence. I know what I'm talking about.
You? Hell, you don't understand the issues.

(But Father, they're killing children).

You got to realize it's all very complicated.
The President knows a lot he doesn't tell the public.
He's our President, he must know what he's doing.
He understands the issues, but you don't.

(But Father, they're killing children).

Take a look around you. Go ahead. Look!
Look at what we got. We live pretty high.
You've always had everything you wanted.
But you just don't understand the issues.

(But Father, they're killing children).

All this stuff didn't come easy, you know.
I had to work all my life to get them.
And we got liberty, free elections, a good GNP.
These are issues you don't understand.

(But Father, they're killing children).

We got to protect what's ours. It's our right.
If we don't stop them there, they'll be over here.
How'd you like that? Them outside on our front lawn?
You just don't understand issues like that.

(But Father, they're killing children).

I just don't understand about you young people these days.
In my day, it was different. We knew what to fight for.
We went over there and kicked hell out of the Jap.
We knew what the issues were all about.

(But Father, they're killing children).

I'd think you'd be proud to go over there and do your part.
It's not just everybody that can have the privilege, you know.
If you weren't my own kid, I'd say you were afraid.
I guess you just don't understand the issues.

(But Father, they're killing children).

By God! I think that's it! You're afraid! My own son!
You and your hippy bastard friends! All of you!
A bunch of no-good fuckin' yellow-bellies!
You don't understand the goddamn issues.

(But Father, they're killing children).

YOU DON'T UNDERSTAND THE ISSUES, YOU SON-OF-A-BITCH!

(But Father, they're killing children).

ashland, 1972

LIFE IS FOR

Life is for
   first of all change
   making love and loving your children
   work which is not to be confused
      with employment
   loneliness and fine company
   hot coffee and letters from friends
   nakedness beside nakedness
   comfort and high risk
   a striving of your own making
   a revealing and sharing of yourself
   the revealing and sharing with yourself
   pain and a going ahead
   the circle of the seasons
Life is for dying
   and not to be afraid.

ashland, 1973

SUICIDE NOTE TO MYSELF

To paint or go mad,
i remember reading that somewhere.
And of course alone again,
a friend of mine had written
that somewhere.

> "I have systematically eliminated
> everything from my life.
> Scotched by conscientious neglect.
> I regret those I leave behind
> but find that insufficient reason
> to continue an existance
> I had no right to wish for."

Instead switch on the light
to note this:
to write now or go mad.

But it is the silences
that must be endured,
the darknesses,
and the things
that disappear.

ashland, 1973

THERE IS A SORROW OUT TONIGHT

There is a sorrow out tonight,
an evil at the center of things,
a fear let loose like sudden convicts,
a death at large in the land.

Happiness is now a forgotten word.
Hope has not been thought of for years.
Love has lost the battles and the war.
The angels have fallen, shot in the heart.

There is a cruelty in the making,
a sickness adrift on the wind,
a weakness spreading like disease,
a loneliness leaping at our throats.

All the struggles and yearnings of the past
have been slaughtered by an instant of hate
and i stand alone in the alley
like a murder waiting to happen.

ashland, 1973

QUESTIONS TO BRECHT

I'd recognize you anywhere, Bertolt.
You with your bowler hat and cigar.
You with your disfigured face
from hatred of misery
and wrath cracking your voice
from too much anger at injustice.
They say you are too negative,
that there's not enough positive
in your work (as if you can be
positive about a madman like Hitler!).
But there is some truth there.

I have seen your children, Bertolt,
covering the shivering tree with sack
and advising them, albeit in sarcasm,
to study mathematics, French, history.
   But where are your women, Bertolt?
You gather them in rocking chairs
no less than you gather men.
What of your wife, Bertolt?
Does she not figure in this?
Marie A is there but only in memory.
Marie Farrar dies in the Meissen Penitentiary.

Lily of Hell drinks too much.
Marie Saunders disappears in Nazi-land.
   But where are your women, Bertolt?
Mother Courage is a woman, right enough.
But did you love her, sleep with her?
Did you laugh with her, marvel at her?
All your women are in agony.
And you suffer greatly for them
but no less than you suffer for all men.
   Where are your women, Bertolt?
Are all of them dead or dying?

I do not attack you, Bertolt.
You said things that I've tried to say.
I, too, know what wisdom is and cannot practice it.
I eat while others starve in chains
and know nothing I do gives me that right.
I know you to be sincere, compassionate.
You were hounded because you thought gently.
You are full of ache for all humanity.
   But where are your women, Bertolt?
Did they get lost in the schemes of politics?
There is no love in you, Bertolt!

ashland, 1973

MEETING IN THE CORNER BAR

Draw'n to an inside straight
ain't what it used to be boy,
he said and sat liver-eyed
over the shot of cheap whisky.
This life ain't what you'd call
a bowl of cheerios. Have another,
he said and poured me a belly-full
of drink to dull the memory.
He looked at me pointedly,
When I was your age, I'd killed
two men. Ya don't believe me, do ya?
I said I had no reason to doubt him.
They was try'n to kill me
was why I done it.
I said I thought that was fine.
I spent thirty-seven years in the navy.
Ya don't believe me, do ya?
Of course I said I did.
That seemed to make him happy.
The Coral Sea, Midway, Okinawa.
Had three destroyers sunk under him.
Kamikazes. Got the DSC.
Korea, too. The Inchon landing.
Shelled the piss outta the gooks
all night and day. Duck soup.
But ending up in a boiler room accident
resultant in a network of scars
and a bevy of gastric disorders.
I ventured that the booze probably
wasn't so good for him.
Hell boy thats whats kept
me alive this long.
Another shot. The bottle gone now.
I may not know much
but I know its goddamn
quiet in this town tonight.
Only the barmaid in the place.
The streets slick with silence.
He had twelve cents left. I had a quarter.
We got two short beers to round out the night.
He looked down at the remaining
seven cents on the table.
Shit, he said. Things is tough
on us old drunks.

ashland, 1973

MARCH 7, 1973

It is my birthday.
I should be excellent.
Accept gifts with boyish hands.
Don't yell at no old ladies,
don't insult no Jehovah's Witnesses,
don't slap no girls on the ass.
I should contemplate my navel,
look myself in the eye,
and, certainly, be in jolly spirits.
Don't get drunk and fall down,
don't punch no holes in the wall,
don't blubber over the last 29 years.
But they have been a bitch!
and I'm goddamn sick of the whole
fucking business.

ashland, 1973

CONCERNING THE WAR

AMONG

THE BREADFRUIT TREES

Jesus! the rich must be some bunch.
They're all well stuffed
like trophy birds.
More fat than I am,
and I look like a glutton
along side all the yellows
and blacks and reds and browns
hungering through the world.

There's a strife on here.
They want something out of me.
But Christ! I've paid my taxes.
I've been a husband, a father.
I've gone to college, joined the union.
I trundled myself off to Asia
like a dutiful little slave.
What more could they possibly want?

All right!

I denounce living!
Isn't that what you bastards want?
Isn't it now? Just isn't it now?

Man of plenty, man of means:
I want to melt down
your rich, upholstered guts!

ashland, 1973

THE COMPOSITION OF A SONG

Come let us make a song
of old men's laughter,
of young girl's yearnings,
of the swallow slung
deep in the sky.

A song where the dead
are exactly happy,
where all the urges
can finally be afforded
and no one thinks
anything of winning.

A song where love
might be given meaning again
and the world is used
like it was always intended.
As a mistress, as a mosque,
as a fetish!

ashland, 1973

FIRST DAY OF SPRING

The first graze of spring
cuts like a bullet sear
across my eyes.
I fear of becoming too small.
It's engulfing, drowning me.
Expressions cross and crack before me
like torn leaves adrift
against the burnished hills.

The birds are nailed to the sky,
black crumbs like dead flies
on the cobalt atmosphere.
Smoke drifts across
the lives we pant after,
tortured like the earth.
A broken-ribbed nagging,
the air like burnt wood.

ashland, 1973

DAINTY BILLY AT WORK IN SAN FRANCISCO

Merry dainty billy
gets cut loose in san francisco.
A company expense account
and businessmen he has to impress.
He'll show them the "now" generation.

The "now" generation does their thing
at north beach flesh joints
and costs $2.50 a drink
(two drinks minimum per show).
Thugs at the door keep you from getting curious.

Merry billy and his colleagues
went nuts over carol doda's swinging boobs,
chicks that made it with elephants
(right there on stage, before your very eyes),
and the marriage of the monkey and the librarian.

They drifted in and out of porno shops
where the gent from sioux bend, idaho
bought a rubberized lady with plastic clit
to be filled with warm water at leisure.
They all thought that was a great joke.

Billy had himself a difficult time
explaining to his troglodyte friends
the evidence of miscegenation on the streets
and all the hopped-up run-aways
that reminded them of their own daughters.

"Everybody's free in san francisco," says billy.
So they strolled in to gawk at the tits
of batgirl, the grandmother of eight, of crazy alma,
and forgot about their daughters in the alleys.
They never understood how bored they were.

Since they were feeling fifteen years younger,
they all wanted a woman but billy drew the line.
He bade them farewell at the san francisco hilton.
And dainty merry billy went back to his apartment
to self-ejaculate to the image of his ex-wife.

ashland, 1973

DAINTY BILLY IN EDEN

Merry dainty billy was at his ease.
A fly-rod in one hand, a beer in the other
and an eye for fish and fowl.

Through a great rent in the sky
the sun swathed its healing rays
and beauty was general in the land.

Spent days hiking a mountain's mountain
from where billy could see
everything in the world worth seeing.

Returned to beth beside the fire,
filled with the enormity of his own churning blood,
to take primitive care with her body.

Then, following a crisis of the mind
(for to live in paradise, one must accept
it unquestioningly--that thing most rare),

billy threw his pole far out in the lake,
no longer listening to what was spoken.
Beth left him for the wilderness and things with more virtue.

Billy, unaffected, took a bite of the apple.
Then God invented
loneliness.

ashland, 1973

DAINTY BILLY REVIEWS HIS LIFE

Merry dainty billy
was somehow vaguely sure
that his life was over.
On one too many occassions
he had acted too slowly
or not slowly enough.
He had been either too passive
or too hostile.
He had suffered sins of omission
or was guilty by design.
There seemed to be
no way out.
And so sitting all day
reading camus, celine, genet
(just the last sort of people
to read when wanting
something to live for)
he knew that this was crisis.
Dainty billy's last attempt
to keep a grip on himself
was when he sat up the whole night
trying to think of something
that would save him.

ashland, 1973

FOR KENNETH PATCHEN

"Let us continue to waste our lives
Declaring beauty to the world ."

Hey, Patchen!
Where are you now?
These guys in America
have nearly forgotten you already.
But they gave you a grand funeral
in San Francisco. All flowers and egos,
reading their poetry to each other.

Hey, Patchen!
One of them said, "When one of us dies
(meaning a poet), it's important for the rest
of us to get together and chant."
So they sang a few "OM's" over your grave
and shrugged home, stuffed full of wine.

Hey, Patchen!
It was a fine eulogy. It would have made you weep.
You who lay shackled to that rack of a bed,
pain-riddled and wasting your life
with only the eternal Miriam beside you,
suffering the poverty and quarantine
reserved for those who don't suck ass,
who are only concerned with truth and justice,
who helped a few of us out of the bog,
who saw with clarity the wretchedness
we cling to with such desperate love.
Whatever I could say now
would indeed be impoverished.

Hey, Patchen!
Wherever you are now
I hope there's cure for a broken back,
and reward for a lasting heart.

ashland, 1973

A BEGINNING

(for DeAnna)

Out of a long cry and tunnel
you have surfaced.
Out of the bleeding that is the world,
out of the leadening nights that look
altogether too goddamn much like death.

(It was a drunken meeting,
with dark eyes colliding
like four strange planets.)

You shift and warm,
smoothing lanquid across the sheets,
swimming in the clustering night,
your hair waterfalling, sheens of brown.

(We have obtained something
here.)

The world is not so very big
but it still has a little space.
Though the smug and hungry face of war
is glinting at the window,
the possibles of love
lie gentle all over the room.

ashland, 1973

DAINTY BILLY IN LOVE

Merry dainty billy (like all of us)
had his troubles with love.
He had gone for years with this blond
when suddenly she didn't want to see him again.

He couldn't seem to get it figured.

He tried everything to woo her back;
from buying her dinner to getting her drunk,
from aphrodisiacs to penis extenders,
from reading her poetry to the roller derby.

Nothing at all remotely worked.

Then in a sheer impotent rage,
billy one night beat the hell out of her.
Spread her brains all over the walls.
The neighbors heard and called the law.

As the police lead him away

merry billy (like all of us)
was reported to have muttered:
"When i was killing her,
at least she wasn't indifferent."

ashland,1973

THE MOON CUT IN SLICES

The pillow was missing your head on it.
Because of that i was bemused
when the landlord demanded my exit.
I wanted to stay among the summer siskiyous,
the land swollen with honey in the sky
but it did, instead, begat a problem.

So a jaunt and spin here and there.
Hitchhikeing around for a taste of future.
Nine hours thumbing on the eugene
off-ramp. No one stopping no one.
But back finally, to the greenry
to blow the dust from a bottle of JD.

So the warm stelth of summer now vague
and the winter oregon's rain slips down
the window like a-many sweatdrops,
the land shrunken, the moon cut in slices.
And, yes, my comely lass,
i did so mighty miss you.

ashland, 1974

DAINTY BILLY GETS EMPLOYED

Merry dainty billy sat in a bar
getting drunk morbidly.
He was busily constructing
tomorrow's hang-over.

ON THIS SITE WILL SOON BE ERECTED
AN HORRENDOUS DRINKING PROBLEM!

Carefully building on the foundations of beer,
the walls went up composed of harder stuff.
The blueprint included fine whisky for the roof
and a lush interior of bourbon.
He was spending money as though he had it.

With such an adept and willing worker,
unlike other major constructions,
the process took only an evening.
Merry dainty billy became even merrier,
pleased with his architecture.

The rafters of tequila went up to the moon,
heavy beams of vodka supported the gin
and the crowds through the knotholes cheered.
The AA sent pickets, threatened to organize
his labor force, but the job went foreward.

"That's not all I'd like to get erected,"
says billy and was out.

Finally, his mind as the sky
as black.
Like all things,
this was built to collapse.

ashland, 1974

FIRST POLITICAL POEM

(for r. m. nixon)

I might just as well
say my bit about Nixon
and be done with it.

Everyone else has.

My friends, I am only thirty
but I remember the 1948 elections.
I was but four years old
and I didn't know what
a President was for.

But I knew that
that was Harry Truman
standing on the back of a train
in our little hamlet
of La Grande, Oregon.

I didn't see Dewey there.

That was the only time our town
ever saw a President, although
Kennedy made a speech there
once when he was Senator.

Nixon never heard of the place.

And I very much doubt if any
future President will ever again
bother about La Grande, Oregon.
Truman was the last of the line.
That is not a happy omen for America.

So I might just as well
say my bit about Nixon
and be done with it.

He's busy preparing his grave.

I remember the Eisenhower-Stevenson
campaigns. Both of them.
That's when I first heard of Nixon.
That was in 1952 and 1956
and--Oh, Lord!--in 1960!

And in California when we thought
we'd rid ourselves of him forever.
Hell, buddy! We ought to have known
the common man can't have _that_ kind of luck.

And of all things, Miami in 1968.
Not only that, but a repeat; circa 1970!

R. M. Nixon has been
in my political consciousness
for as long as I've had
a political consciousness.

Ergo! I might just as well
say my bit about Nixon
and be done with it.

I've hated the son-of-a-bitch
all my waking, quaking life!

san francisco, 7/31/1974

HOMAGE TO DOCTOR BERRYMAN (1914-1972)

There are many who touch.
Few scor ch.

Mr. Alvarez, Sir, you are wrong.
It is worth the terrible cost.
Since John would have suffered
in any case, whether artist
(whatever nebulous thing)
or just a living man

should he not then have tried
to do something durable?
Not every alcoholic is a poet.
Not every suicide, a creative genius.
Though his skull rang with his end;
he runs on still, love for love.

John was a wild bad father.
But John simply didn't have choice.

The facts & issues are clear.
He followed Plath. (Sexton has
newly arrived.) Joined Wang Wei.
The pretty soon became the now.
His meeting with Thomas,
like Henry's nocturnal habits,

was the terror not only of their women,
but of the entire Seattle.
But John won't down a-many few
with Dylan or anyone, anymore.
As traveler, he took the same train
that the others took, to the same place.

John had strange singing dreams.
Pried himself open for all the world to see.

If even Henry bored him, Mr. Bones,
what hope was there?
Christ did not come riding to rescue.
If anything, He made it more difficult
and was, after the last, of pitiful use.
No accident John's finale was Delusions, etc.

With no way to escape reality from delusion,
he didn't feel that Will change.
There was never any Recovery.
They will never leave
John alone with his insights.
The mighty men encamped against him.

And there was indeed a law
against John.

san francisco, 1974